**Discovering
Cultures**

Jamaica

Jennifer Rozines Roy and Gregory Roy

MARSHALL CAVENDISH
NEW YORK

With thanks to Dr. Carlene J. Edie, Professor, Department of Political Science,
University of Massachusetts at Amherst, for the careful review of this manuscript.

Marshall Cavendish
99 White Plains Road
Tarrytown, New York 10591-9001
www.marshallcavendish.com

Library of Congress Cataloging-in-Publication Data

Roy, Jennifer Rozines, 1967–
Jamaica / by Jennifer Rozines Roy and Gregory Roy.
p. cm. — (Discovering cultures)
Includes bibliographical references and index.
ISBN 0-7614-1793-1
1. Jamaica—Juvenile literature. I. Roy, Gregory. II. Title. III. Series.
F1868.2.R69 2004
972.92—dc22   2004006142

Photo Research by Candlepants Incorporated
Cover Photo: Nik Wheeler/Corbis

The photographs in this book are used by permission and through the courtesy of; *Corbis*: Howard Davies, 1, 21; David Cumming; Eye Ubiquitous, 4, 14, 26, 36; Sergio Pitamitz, 6-7; Tim Thompson, 10; Jan Butchofsky-Houser, 19 (top); Reuters, 30, 31, 45; Jeremy Horner, 32; Tim Graham, 34; Michael Freeman, 39; Underwood & Underwood, 44 (top right). *The Image Works*: UNEP/Topham, 8, 42 (lower right); Jeff Greenberg, 19 (lower), 24, 43 (lower right); Hinata Haga/HAGA, 35, 38, 43 (top left), Topham/Picturepoint, 44 (lower left). *Getty Images*: Melanie Acevedo, 12; PhotoDisc Green, 13, 16; Gen Nishino, 15, 29, back cover. *Danita Delimont Stock Photography*: Jon Arnold, 9; Randa Bishop, 20. *Bernard St. Aubyn/Photo Researchers Inc.*: 11, 43 (lower left). *Bruce Coleman Inc.*: John Guistina, 18; Lee Foster, 22; Werner J. Bertsch, 37. *Index Stock Imagery*: Michael Siluk, 25 (both); Beverly Factor, 28.

Cover: *Cliff on the Jamaican coast*; Title page: *Jamaican children*

Map and illustrations by Ian Warpole
Book design by Virginia Pope

Printed in China
1 3 5 6 4 2

Turn the Pages...

Where in the World Is Jamaica?

Jamaica is an island in the Caribbean Sea. It is located between North America and South America among a group of islands called the West Indies. It is a small country, just about the size of Connecticut.

Jamaica has a tropical climate. It is hot and humid year-round. It never gets very cold on the island. In the summer the average temperature is 80 degrees Fahrenheit (26 degrees Celsius), and in the winter it is 75 degrees Fahrenheit (23 degrees Celsius).

While it always feels warm in Jamaica, winds often blow in from the sea making the air a bit cooler. The winds are called the "doctor breeze" because they make people feel better.

Boats docked on a Jamaican beach

Map of Jamaica

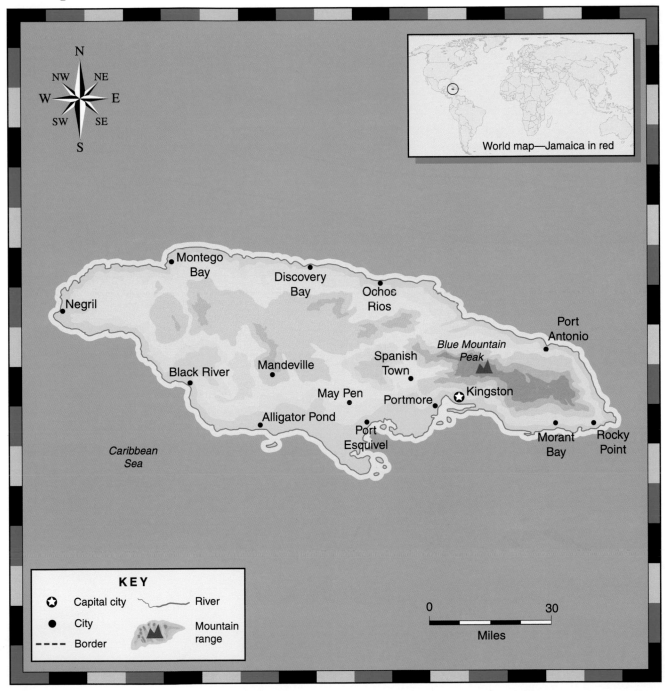

World map—Jamaica in red

Montego Bay
Discovery Bay
Ochos Rios
Negril
Port Antonio
Blue Mountain Peak
Black River
Mandeville
Spanish Town
May Pen
Portmore
Kingston
Alligator Pond
Port Esquivel
Morant Bay
Rocky Point
Caribbean Sea

KEY

⊛ Capital city   River

● City   Mountain range

– – – Border

0   30
Miles

The sun shines often on Jamaica. There is, however, a rainy season from June to November. During this time there are sudden, heavy rains and strong winds, especially in the northern part of the island. Jamaica lies in the Caribbean's "hurricane belt." Hurricanes are storms with damaging winds and flooding rains. While most rainstorms are not dangerous, hurricanes can destroy buildings and hurt or kill people. Fortunately, hurricanes do not strike very often. Overall, the weather on Jamaica is calm and delightful.

Jamaica's geography looks quite different as you travel around the island. In the central part, there are thick green forests, waterfalls, and caves. Along the coast there are miles and miles of sandy beaches.

Most of Jamaica, though, is hilly. The Blue Mountains rise above the eastern region and include Jamaica's highest point, Blue Mountain Peak. It is 7,402 feet (2,257 meters) above sea level. The steep mountains have a blue misty fog floating around them, making them quite a sight to see.

Waterfalls in the forest of central Jamaica

The Blue Mountains rise high over the island.

Many rivers flow through Jamaica. Sometimes after heavy rains they flood over their banks. Many years ago, Jamaicans traveled up and down these rivers on bamboo rafts delivering goods to different towns and ports. Today, guides take visitors on boat tours along the waters to view the beautiful greenery and tropical birds.

The surface of much of the island is made up of a rock called limestone. In some places, the limestone is covered by thick red soil that contains bauxite. Bauxite is the main source of aluminum, which is a metal used in cans, cars, foil, and many everyday objects. Jamaican bauxite is sold to other countries.

Agriculture is also a very important part of Jamaica's economy. Jamaica's tropical climate is very good for growing sugarcane, bananas, coconuts, and coffee. Jamaican farmers work very hard collecting these crops, which are sold to stores and food companies around the world.

Jamaica's largest source of income is tourism. Every year, more than a million people from different countries travel to Jamaica to enjoy the sunshine, sandy beaches, and tropical rain forests. There are vacation resorts on many beaches where visitors can swim, snorkel, sail, and soak up the sunshine. The largest tourist destination is Montego Bay, also known as Mo' Bay. Other popular tourist towns are Ocho Rios and Negril.

Jamaica's capital city is Kingston, which sits between a mountain range and a waterfront harbor in the southeastern corner of the island. Kingston is home to one-third of Jamaica's population, making it the country's largest city. After an earthquake in 1907 ruined much of the area, Kingston was rebuilt. Today it is the country's business and cultural center. Kingston has tall buildings, museums, art galleries, restaurants, and food markets. The streets are busy with buses, cars, and people.

Spanish Town was the capital of Jamaica from 1662 to 1872. Founded by the Spanish, it remained the capital city even after Jamaica became a British colony.

Spanish Town contains many buildings important to Jamaica's history. It is also the location of the People's Museum, which has displays on Jamaican architecture, agriculture, crafts, and traditions.

A view of downtown Kingston

While its cities may be crowded, much of Jamaica is rural and filled with nature. Lush green forests contain a variety of plants, animals, and birds. Jamaica has over 3,000 species of flowers—800 of which are found nowhere else in the world.

The hilly countryside

The forest is also home to many wild creatures including crocodiles, mongoose, large lizards, spiders, and bats, known as "rat-bats." And if you look up in the trees, you may spot colorful parrots and owls.

Along the coast of the Caribbean Sea is an incredible underwater world. There are fish darting in and out of the coral reefs, as well as turtles, sharks, manta rays, and manatees.

Unfortunately, Jamaica's natural resources have not always been well cared for. The development of hotels and resorts has torn up many beaches, and loggers have cut down thousands of forest trees. The natural habitats of many animals have been destroyed.

Today, Jamaica is working to protect its environment. There are national parks that preserve endangered species, botanical gardens that grow tropical plants, and marine parks that protect sea life.

The Doctor Bird

Shiny and tiny, the streamer-tailed hummingbird is Jamaica's national bird. It is found only in Jamaica. It is nicknamed the "doctor bird," perhaps because its black cap and tails resemble the top hat and long-tailed coat doctors used to wear. The doctor bird's feathers are iridescent green and unlike the feathers of any other bird in the world. The male doctor bird has two long tails that flow out behind him when he flies. The doctor bird is pictured on the Jamaican dollar bill and is considered a symbol of the uniqueness of the country. Some Jamaicans believe that the bird has magical powers. This is shown in a folk song that says, "Doctor bud a cunny bud, hard bud fe dead." This means: The doctor bird is a clever bird, which cannot be killed easily.

What Makes Jamaica Jamaican?

Jamaican culture is truly unique. It combines traditions from its history with a lifestyle that is easygoing and relaxed. The Jamaican people are proud to be from their island and have as their national motto: "Out of many, one people." This motto reflects the country's many different peoples—Africans, East Indians, Chinese, Europeans, Syrians, and Lebanese—and how they all come together as Jamaicans.

More than two and one-half million people live in Jamaica. The Spanish ruled Jamaica from 1494–1666. The British ruled from 1666–1962. Most Jamaicans (more than 90 percent) are from families that lived in Africa until the seventeenth or eighteenth century. That was when the British, who

Smiling in the Jamaican sunshine

ruled Jamaica during that time, captured thousands of Africans and brought them to the island. The African slaves worked the land and had very hard lives. In 1838, all the slaves were set free. In 1962, Jamaica became an independent country within the British Commonwealth of Nations.

Today, Jamaica is a blend of its African and British backgrounds. It is an independent state and is ruled by a Jamaican prime minister. The official language is

This man wears his hair in dreadlocks.

A Rastafarian family in the doorway of their house

English. In businesses and schools, people speak English. But at home and on the streets, Jamaicans speak *patois.* Patois is a mixture of English, different African languages, and Spanish that is spoken in a singsong style. To outsiders, patois can be difficult to understand.

Jamaicans move at a slower pace than many other people in the world. Perhaps it is because of the heat, or maybe it is just the nature of its people, but nobody seems to rush in Jamaica. The clothing people wear is also casual. Jamaicans wear short-sleeved shirts with light pants or shorts, or summery dresses. On Sundays, they dress up for church.

An important part of Jamaican life is religion. Most Jamaicans are Christians. They attend Christian churches and celebrate Christian holidays. However, some Jamaicans follow religions based on African beliefs. These people believe that spirits can be used to influence the human world. Folk healers who practice these religions use native plants to heal the sick and perform rituals to chase away evil spirits. Rastafarianism is a religion that is based on African pride. Many *Rastafarians* wear their uncombed hair in twisted rows called dreadlocks or "dreads."

Jamaican culture is a mixture of old African traditions and new Caribbean ones. The arts are very important in Jamaican life. Music seems to be everywhere—on buses, in stores, and out on the streets. Loudspeakers blast Jamaican music in village squares, and people often sing and dance along. Jamaican music has a strong drumbeat and a bouncy rhythm just right for dancing!

Playing the banjo and whistling a tune

Arts and crafts have also become popular on the island. Jamaican artists carve beautiful sculptures, dishes, and masks from local wood. Jamaican paintings are often very colorful and show scenes of Jamaican life or landscapes. In towns such as Kingston, large paintings cover the outside walls of buildings.

Jamaicans enjoy watching poets perform dub poetry. Dub poetry comes from the African folk tradition of telling stories that are passed on from generation to generation. Dub poets speak in patois to a rhythmic beat or to music. The poems can be about anything from life in Jamaica today to the performer's feelings or the telling of an old folktale. Whatever the subject, the people watching often yell, clap, and drum along with the dub poet.

Faces of Jamaicans carved in wood

Reggae Music

Jamaican *reggae* music is world famous. Reggae musicians play electric guitars and drum to an island rhythm. The songs are sung in patois and are usually about love, peace, and harmony.

Reggae was made popular by Rastafarians. For Rastafarians, music, including reggae, is used to express their faith.

Today, reggae is popular with people of all ages and faiths. Every year, thousands of people from many different countries come to Jamaica to celebrate the Reggae Sunsplash music festival. Reggae bands perform on stage or right on the beach as huge crowds sing and dance to the reggae beat.

Living in Jamaica

Sunrise over a rural home

In the rural areas, most families live in traditional Jamaican houses. The homes are small, with tin roofs and wooden walls. The outsides of the houses are often painted in bright colors such as red or green. Some rural families have small farms where they grow fruit and vegetables and keep pigs, chickens, and goats. In some villages, people do not have electricity or running water inside their homes.

In towns like Kingston and Montego Bay, there are middle-class suburbs. The

Bicycling through
a shantytown

homes are larger and more modern. Middle-class families have the same things that people living in the United States do, such as cars, home computers, and CD players. The wealthiest people live in beautiful luxury homes.

There are also many poor areas called shantytowns, where tiny shacks are crowded together on the streets.

Daily life in Jamaica differs depending on where a person lives. Jamaicans who live in the suburbs are very much like middle-class American families. They work at interesting jobs, wear the latest fashions, and shop in supermarkets. However, the majority of Jamaican people do not live like this.

A busy street in Port Antonio

Compared with the United States, the countries of the Caribbean are poor. One-third of Jamaica's families are poor, and many adults cannot find jobs. Those who do work often have low-paying jobs in hotels or restaurants that cater to tourists. Some men leave their families for months at a time to work in the city or in other countries. Other families earn money by selling *ganja* (marijuana), a drug that is illegal but widely used around the country.

Jamaica is a matriarchal society. This means that the women make decisions at home and take on the responsibilities of raising the family. Many Jamaican men expect girls and women to do the cooking, housework, childcare, and to also make money. Men are often expected to be "macho," and boys learn to act tough. However, many families are loving and happy, with polite, well-behaved children. Jamaican families are often large, with many children, grandparents, and other relatives all living together.

A saleswoman at a craft market

No matter where Jamaicans live, they all have one thing in common—they enjoy good food! Nobody goes hungry in Jamaica. Even the poorest country folk can pick fresh bananas and coconuts from the trees and catch tasty fish from the rivers.

Serving up salt fish and ackee

The most popular seafood dish is salt fish and *ackee*. A heavily salted fish is served with ackee, a fruit that looks like scrambled eggs when it is cooked. Jamaicans are careful to cook only ripe ackee, because the fruit can be poisonous if not prepared correctly.

Jamaicans like their food spicy. Jerk is a favorite style of cooking. Spicy jerk seasoning is used to coat meat or chicken, which is then barbecued on a grill or over a fire pit. Many Jamaicans also enjoy curried goat, which is so hot and spicy it can burn your mouth. The most popular snack is a patty of spicy meat wrapped in a crust.

Other common foods in Jamaica are yams, rice and red beans (called peas), and bammy, a pancake-shaped bread. Fresh fruits such as papayas,

This platter of fresh fruit looks healthy and delicious.

mangoes, and coconuts are enjoyed year-round. *Plantains*, a kind of green banana, are cooked in desserts or fried into chips for snacking.

Jamaicans buy their food from supermarkets or from outdoor markets or street vendors. Most towns have a town square, which is usually busy with people shopping for bargains on food, crafts, and other wares.

A special time for Jamaican families is Sunday dinner. Relatives gather each week to eat a large meal and to enjoy each other's company. In patois, the word *nyam* means eat. With all the delicious food on the island, it is no wonder Jamaicans love to nyam!

Let's Eat!
Jamaican Rock Buns

Here is a recipe for tasty Jamaican rolls. They include spices, but they are sweet instead of hot. Make sure you have an adult's help when you use the oven, and wash your hands before you begin.

3 teaspoons butter

1/2 cup sugar

1 large egg, beaten

1 teaspoon vanilla

1 1/2 cups flour

1 teaspoon baking powder

1/2 cup raisins

pinch each of nutmeg
and cinnamon

1. Mix together butter and sugar

2. Add egg and vanilla

3. Stir in flour, baking powder, raisins, nutmeg, and cinnamon

4. Form round buns and place on cookie sheet

5. Bake at 350 degrees Fahrenheit (177 degrees Celsius) until lightly browned

6. Let cool a bit, then nyam!

School Days

Before Jamaica's independence in 1962, only the rich children were educated. Since then, the Jamaican government has worked hard to build schools for everyone. Today, children all over the island go to free public schools. There are also private schools where families pay fees for their children's education.

Jamaican children begin school when they are six years old. They learn subjects like reading, writing, math, computers, and Bible studies. In school, students and teachers speak English, not patois.

Inside the classroom, a student who has just taken a difficult exam might say, "Boy! I thought that test would have been easy." But when he goes outside and hangs out with his buddies, he would complain, "Bwaay! Mi did tink de test was easy."

Jamaican children wear uniforms to school. The school day starts at about eight o'clock in the morning and lasts until one o'clock or one thirty in the afternoon. After that, there is always homework to do! Some students stay later to take extra classes or to get additional help. Schoolteachers can be very strict with students, and children get punished if they do not behave.

Students wearing school uniforms

Young students enjoying their lunch

When children are ten or eleven, they all take an exam. Students who perform well on this test can continue on to secondary school, or high school. These students' names are published in the newspaper, and their families are very proud. Girls and boys who attend high school take their education very seriously. They study hard with the hope of going to college or to a vocational school that teaches skills like carpentry or home economics.

Only about half of all Jamaican children go on to high school, however. Many students drop out of elementary school when they are twelve or thirteen. Just like in other parts of life on the island, there is a big difference

Taking a test seems a little nicer outdoors.

between the education of the rich and the poor. High school students are often from wealthier families. Schools in poor areas are very crowded, and they do not have enough books, supplies, or good teachers. Children from primary schools in rural areas or in city slums often do not get a good enough education to pass the exam to get into high school. Those who do pass may drop out anyway, because they do not have enough money for high school uniforms, books, or other supplies.

Students who leave school at a young age usually try to find work to help support their families. But the jobs they find are hard and do not pay much. By the time they become young adults, they may have given up on having a successful future. In recent years, the Jamaican government has offered classes that teach reading, writing, and computer skills to adults, which helps them to find better work and to live better lives.

A boy smiles over his schoolwork.

The National Song for Schools

The Jamaican national song is sung by schoolchildren to show their pride and loyalty to their country.

Just for Fun

What do Jamaican children do with their free time? They have lots of fun! They enjoy playing video games, listening to music, using the computer, and watching television. They watch TV shows and movies from England and the U.S. as well as from Jamaica. However, because the weather is usually so nice, Jamaican kids spend much of their time playing outside.

Jamaicans of all ages enjoy sports. Football, called soccer in the United States, basketball, and baseball are popular. Children play and compete in youth leagues after school and on weekends. The favorite sport is *cricket*. Cricket was brought to Jamaica by the British. Many boys dream of becoming cricket players for the famous West Indies team and playing against the best teams

Children playing together on the beach

Jumping from rock to rock in the lake

around the world. On days when there is a big cricket match, it seems the whole country is excited. Thousands of Jamaicans watch the games from the sports arena or on television at home.

Two soccer players fight for the ball.

While young cricket players are mostly boys, there are plenty of sports that Jamaican girls enjoy. Girls play a type of basketball game in which the ball cannot touch the ground—no dribbling. They also play Dandy Shandy, a game during

Jamaican athletes jump hurdles to lead the pack.

which the pitchers throw a stuffed cardboard box called the "ball." The pitchers try to hit another player, who must jump and duck to avoid getting out. Another girls' activity that involves jumping is jumping rope. Girls can skip so fast that the rope becomes a blur!

Jamaican kids love to run races. They race in the schoolyard at recess and train in track and field when school is out. Running is a popular pastime for adults, too. Jamaica's track and field athletes are world-class. Jamaican runners have won medals at the Olympics.

A popular indoor game among Jamaicans is dominoes. Children are taught to play the game, which uses light-colored tiles with black dots, in school. Many men and boys meet in shops or community rooms to play. A good dominoes player must think quickly and use smart strategies to win the game.

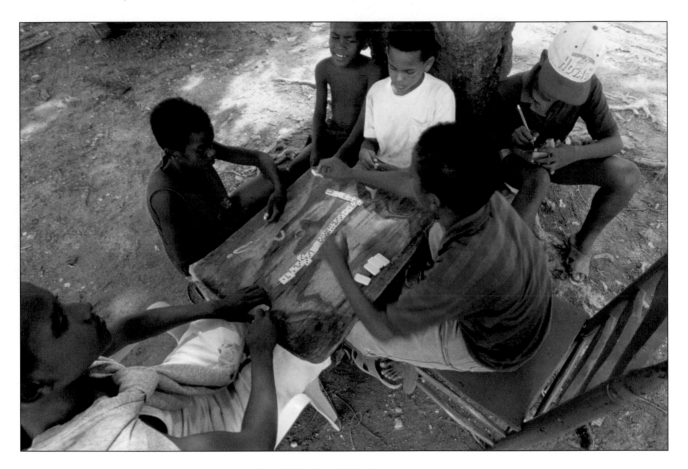

A neighborhood dominoes game

Cricket

What is Jamaica's national sport? It is cricket! Cricket is played on a field that is about 550 feet long. In the center of the field is a small area called the pitch. It has two wooden frames called wickets. Two teams of eleven players compete. In cricket, just as in baseball, one entire team goes out onto the field while individual players from the other team come to bat.

The batsman, or batter, has two jobs. He must protect the wicket from being knocked over by a ball thrown by a pitcher, called a bowler. He also tries to hit the ball with his bat. When the batsman hits the ball, it can go in any direction—including behind him. Then the batsman runs to the far end of the pitch to the other wicket to score a run. Depending on how far the ball went, he may get an even higher score.

When the match gets going, it can be really exciting. The bowler might throw a fast "googly" (spinner) that gets whacked out of the cricket field by the batsman, who then scores six runs for his team. Meanwhile, fans in the audience scream, cheer, and boo.

A great day for a batsman is one in which he reaches a "century" — one hundred runs. But if he does not score a single run, he has been "bowled for a duck"—a cricket player's worst nightmare!

Let's Celebrate!

Colorful costumes, loud music, dancing in the streets—it is celebration time in Jamaica! Jamaicans love a good party, and they celebrate many special days throughout the year.

Most Jamaicans are Christians, and Christian holidays are very important to Jamaican families. They go to church and observe religious traditions.

Christmas is a major celebration in Jamaica. Christmas preparations begin weeks ahead of time. Women clean out their homes and begin making food for family gatherings. In the small towns and villages, people of all ages practice dance moves and songs for the Jonkonnu, an African Christmas festival that is celebrated all over the Caribbean and in Africa.

Dancers wear costumes in the colors of the Jamaican flag.

The Jonkonnu begins with a big parade. Musicians playing drums and small flutes march in the parade. People dress up in colorful costumes and masks and dance through streets. The costumes can be funny or scary. There are animals, kings, queens, and devils. One of the craziest-looking characters is the Pitchy-Patchy Man. His costume is made of long strips of colorful cloth that swing from side to side as he dances.

Christmastime on a street in Montego Bay

After the Jonkonnu parade, people enjoy more singing and dancing. Then, everyone goes home for a delicious holiday meal.

Also taking place around Christmastime is the Jamaican *pantomime*. Performers act out stories and perform dances during the pantomime festival. Some of the shows make fun of Jamaican politicians and current events. People in the audience shout out jokes and remarks about the performance.

In the cities, Santa Claus is a part of Christmas. And just like in the United States, many Jamaican children receive gifts and treats for Christmas. However, some families do not exchange presents because they believe Christmas is strictly a religious time, or because they are too poor to buy gifts.

Still, all around Jamaica you will hear Christmas carols. They can be sung the traditional American way or performed with a Jamaican twist—reggae style.

The biggest celebration in Jamaica takes place in August. It is Independence Day. This festival marks the time when Jamaica became an independent country. Schoolchildren learn about their country's history and culture. While they get ready for this holiday, they practice songs, dances, and plays that celebrate Jamaica's spirit.

Independence Day festivals take place all over the island, but the biggest one is held in Kingston. On the morning of the big day, awards are given to people who have contributed good things to their communities. Then there is a parade of decorated floats. Some parade marchers dress up as "Big Heads," which are giant costume heads that represent famous Jamaicans.

Dressing up like a clown for a festival

In the afternoon, there are lively performances and games. Many people dance around a maypole, a tall pole decorated with colorful streamers. As with other Jamaican festivals, Independence Day is celebrated with lots of music, food, and drink. Adults enjoy punch mixed with rum—a popular drink made in Jamaica. Children cool off by eating sno-cones, which are treats made of shaved or crushed ice covered with flavored syrups.

Another celebration related to Jamaica's history is the Maroon Festival. It takes place in "Cockpit Country," an area in the hills where the *Maroons* live. The Maroons are descendants of slaves who ran

Celebrating is lots of fun with friends.

Musicians play for the crowds during the Maroon Festival.

away from their owners to live in the hills. People come from all over the island to celebrate the slaves' escape from their cruel masters. Ceremonies are also held to remember the signing of a peace treaty with the British.

During the Maroon Festival, people dress in costumes and rub ashes on their faces. Musicians sing and dance to traditional songs with African rhythms and drumbeats. A special horn called the *abeng* is played. The Maroons sing songs to honor Cudjoe, a brave leader of the runaway slaves. Other songs are about Nanny of the Maroons, a woman who fought for her people against the British.

Of course, no Jamaican celebration is complete without food. The whole community finishes off the Maroon Festival with a big barbecue feast.

Whether it is held in a downtown city street or a small village in the country, a Jamaican celebration means fun and excitement for everyone!

Carnival

Put on your costumes and masks and get ready for a big party! It is Carnival time in Jamaica!

In April, just before the religious season of Lent, Jamaicans celebrate a weeklong festival called Carnival. There are street parades with floats and entertainers. People dress up in crazy, colorful outfits. There is even a "Kiddies' Carnival" just for the children. There are games and prizes and costume contests.

The main music played at Carnival is soca music. Soul Calypso, or soca, is a music with a strong beat and Caribbean sound.

The Jamaican Carnival first took place in 1990. It has quickly become one of the biggest events on the island. It is one of the few times when all people—rich, poor, old, young, Jamaicans, and tourists—come together to celebrate. At Carnival, many people say, there are no prejudices or bad feelings. There is only peace, love, and lots of fun.

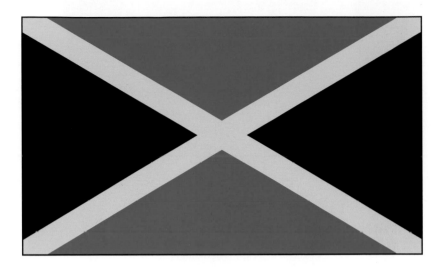

The Jamaican national flag shows a diagonal cross with four triangles. The green stands for hope and agricultural resources; black for strength and hardships overcome; and yellow for natural wealth and sunshine.

Jamaicans use Jamaican dollars. They use coins and paper bills with pictures of famous Jamaican people on them. In May 2004, about sixty Jamaican dollars equaled one U.S. dollar.

Glossary

ackee A Jamaican fruit.

cricket A game played with a ball and bat between two competing teams.

ganja An illegal drug. Also called marijuana.

Maroons Escaped slaves who lived in the mountains and hills, also the name of their living descendants.

pantomime The telling of a story without talking, using body movements and facial expressions.

patois A language that combines English words with Jamaican words and phrases.

plantain A type of green banana that must be cooked before being eaten.

Rastafarian A member of a religious group based on African pride.

reggae A popular Jamaican music with a strong beat and meaningful lyrics.

shantytowns Areas of poor homes located at the edge of a city.

Fast Facts

Jamaica is an island in the Caribbean Sea. It is located between North America and South America among a group of islands called the West Indies.

Montego Bay
Discovery Bay
Ochos Rios
Negril
Port Antonio
Blue Mountain Peak
Spanish Town
Black River
Mandeville
May Pen
Portmore
Kingston
Alligator Pond
Port Esquivel
Morant Bay
Rocky Point

Jamaica's capital city is Kingston. Kingston is home to one-third of Jamaica's population, making it the country's largest city

Jamaica is an independent state within the British Commonwealth of Nations. It is ruled by a Jamaican prime minister.

The Blue Mountains include Jamaica's highest point, Blue Mountain Peak. It is 7,402 feet (2,257 m) above sea level.

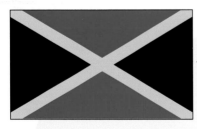

The Jamaican national flag shows a diagonal cross with four triangles. The green stands for hope and agricultural resources; black for strength and hardships overcome; and yellow for natural wealth and sunshine.

42

In Jamaica,
61 percent of the
people are Protestant,
4 percent are Roman
Catholic, and
35 percent are other
religions.

Jamaicans use
Jamaican dollars. In
May 2004, about sixty
Jamaican dollars
equaled one U.S.
dollar.

English is
the official
language of
Jamaica.

Shiny and tiny, the
streamer-tailed hummingbird is
Jamaica's national bird. It is found
only in Jamaica. It is nicknamed
the "doctor bird."

As of July
2003, there
were 2,695,867
people living in
Jamaica.

The Jamaican national motto
is: "Out of many, one people." This motto
reflects the country's many different peoples—
Africans, East Indians, Chinese, Europeans,
Syrians, and Lebanese.

Proud to Be Jamaican

Marcus Mosiah Garvey (1887–1940)

Marcus Mosiah Garvey was one of the most powerful leaders of the black rights movement of the twentieth century. After working as a printer and seeing how poorly black workers were treated, he founded the Universal Negro Improvement Association. His goal was to give people dignity and to change policies that kept blacks from living successful lives.

Garvey also started the "Back to Africa" movement and believed that black people should move back to their African homeland. However, he also made great efforts to improve the lives of blacks wherever they lived. His organization grew to 12 million members around the world and inspired black politicians, musicians, and businessmen to achieve great things.

Bob Marley (1945–1981)

Bob Marley was a musician known for bringing reggae music to the world. He and his band, the Wailers, had many hit songs and sold millions of albums. Marley's music combined African rhythms and drums with the electric guitar. The words he sang were often about peace, love, and togetherness.

Bob Marley was born in a tiny village and spent his teenage years in Trench Town, a Kingston ghetto. He was a Rastafarian who wore his hair in long dreadlocks. Like many Rastafarians, he was against violence and injustice. Although Bob Marley was a wealthy superstar, he never forgot his humble roots. He always spoke of Jamaica with great pride and love.

Marley died of cancer in 1981. He was awarded the Order of Merit, Jamaica's highest honor. He was buried with his guitar in a crypt right next to the one-room cottage where he grew up.

Merlene Ottey (1960–)

Merlene Ottey is the most famous female athlete in Jamaica, and is considered to be one of the most successful track and field stars of all time. Ottey was born in a poor village in the Jamaican countryside. She began competing in races when she was thirteen years old. She trained for years and made it to the Olympics when she was twenty years old.

In 1980, Ottey became the first Jamaican to win an Olympic medal. She was best in the sprint events like the 100- and 200-meter races. Sprinters must run very fast over short distances, and Merlene Ottey was one of the fastest sprinters in the world. She won six more medals in later Olympic games and a record fourteen medals in World Championships.

Find Out More

Books

Festivals of the World: Jamaica by Robert Barlas. Gareth Stevens Publishing, Milwaukee, Wisconsin, 1998.

Jamaica by Frances Wilkins. Chelsea House Publishers, Hong Kong, 1999.

Picture a Country: Jamaica by Henry Pluckrose. Franklin Watts, Danbury, Connecticut, 1998.

A Ticket to Jamaica by Michael Capek. Carolrhoda Books, Minneapolis, Minnesota, 1999.

We Come from Jamaica by Alison Brownlie. Steck-Vaughn, Austin, Texas, 2000.

Web Sites*

http://www.jamaicans.com/childsguide/
A kids' guide to Jamaica that includes information on people, children, food, language, history, geography, music, activities, and more.

http://www.jamaicatravel.com
A travel guide for visitors, vacationers, and anyone interested in what Jamaica has to offer, including island news.

Video

Jamaica. AAA Travel Video Series. 1995.

*All Internet sites were available and accurate when sent to press.

Index

Page numbers for illustrations are in **boldface.**

About the Authors

Jennifer Rozines Roy is the author of more than twenty books, including three for Benchmark Books. A former Gifted and Talented teacher, she holds a B.S. in psychology and an M.A. in elementary education.

Gregory Roy has co-authored three books with his wife. He holds a B.S. in civil engineering, manages a branch office of a national engineering firm, and has always held an interest in all things Jamaican. The Roys live in upstate New York with their son Adam.